W9-BRY-861

God's Images

GOD'S IMAGES

The Bible: A New Vision

JAMES DICKEY & MARVIN HAYES

A CROSSROAD BOOK • THE SEABURY PRESS • NEW YORK

1978
THE SEABURY PRESS
815 Second Avenue, New York, N.Y. 10017

GOD'S IMAGES
A Crossroad Book published by arrangement with Oxmoor House, Inc.
The Oxmoor House edition published September 1977
The Seabury Press edition published September 1978

Copyright © 1977 by Oxmoor House, Inc.
Text copyright © 1978 by James Dickey
All rights reserved. No part of this book may be reproduced, stored in a
retrieval system, or transmitted, in any form or by any means, electronic,
mechanical, photocopying, recording, or otherwise, without permission.
For information address: Oxmoor House, Inc., P.O. Box 2463,
Birmingham, Alabama 35202.

Printed in the United States of America

Library of Congress Cataloging in Publication Data

Dickey, James.   God's Images: the Bible: a new vision
"A Crossroad book."
1. Bible—Meditations. 2. Bible—Illustrations. 3. Prose Poems,
American. I. Hayes, Marvin. II. Title.
BS491.5.D52   1978   811'.5'4   78-17465   ISBN 0-8164-2194-3 pbk.

Advisory Board for GOD'S IMAGES

   Keith Crim, Ph.D., General Editor, *Supplementary Volume, The
Interpreter's Dictionary of the Bible*; Professor of Philosophy and Religious
Studies, Virginia Commonwealth University, Richmond, Virginia
   Hubert H. Harper, Jr. Ph.D., Associate Dean of the Graduate School,
University of Alabama in Birmingham, Alabama
   Father Roland E. Murphy, O. Carm., Professor of Religion, The
Divinity School, Duke University, Durham, North Carolina
   Harry M. Orlinsky, Ph.D., Effie Wise Ochs Professor of Bible, Hebrew
Union College—Jewish Institute of Religion, New York, New York
   Malcolm L. Peel, Ph.D., Chairman and Professor of Religion, Coe
College, Cedar Rapids, Iowa

Foreword

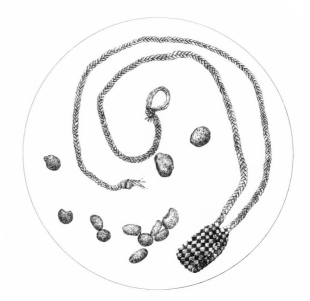

The Bible is the greatest treasure-house of powerful, disturbing, life-enhancing images in the whole of humanity's long history. They are the images of what generations of men have taken to be those projected on the human race by God Himself, or God as He resides in the souls of men. To an artist such as Marvin Hayes, or to a poet, such as I hold myself to be, these images have unfolded in us by means of the arts we practice. These are *our* images of *God's Images*. Each man, each woman, each child has his own interpretation of these unforgettable scenes, and, inevitably, his own personal reenactment of them. All of us, while sleeping, have felt the strength leave us, as our hair is cut away. This time, we are Samson. This time, too, we have been the woman, as with exquisite delicacy she shears the strength-bestowing hair. As we read we understand the strange sleep-loss of power and understand also why and how the woman is acting as she does. We have felt the warm glow on our shoulders of Joseph's coat of many colors, and we turn to salt with Lot's wife each time we enter the ocean and taste it.

We all have our images of God, given to us by the Bible, which is the Word of God. These images are ours, and in calling them up in our minds we are living witnesses of the fact that "the kingdom of God is within you."

These then, in this book, are some of the images from the inner kingdoms of two men, one an artist, the other a poet. Marvin Hayes's etchings are his pictorial record of his personal kingdom of God. The prose poems I write, about the same episodes he illustrates, are *my* kingdom, shown forth, as best I can do, in the medium of words. Hayes and I do not wish to supersede or in any way substitute our interpretations of the Bible for yours. These are crucial to you, and therefore vital and living. We should like to think, though, that we may be able to give an added dimension to your own inner Bible and enrich your personal kingdom of God, there where it lies forever . . . within you.

Marvin Hayes is a visionary artist. He, as in the case of his great predecessor, William Blake, has "kept the Divine Vision in time of trouble." All visionaries are unique, and though Hayes admires Blake, he goes his own way into that realm where the eye, the hand, and the imagination coincide in extraordinary ways to produce *God's Images*.

In doing so Hayes has added a cubit to our stature of imagination about these things that matter to us most, and has done this by the imagination of the poet which is the essential imagination of the Bible, whether 2000 years ago or now. No one can see Hayes's etchings without having his vision of these essential matters of our world, shift.

How does Hayes make this happen? How do the human eye, mind and hand cause these forms of men and women, of landscape and beast and building, to come forth before us as though the human beings were speaking shadows, with the haunted reality of shadows, yet with the timed joy and timeless griefs of mortal and immortal flesh? Hayes works with small, almost infinitely small, gradations; he cross-stitches in smooth metal, with acids and cutting, inked troughs, the fabulous world we all have fallen from, and toward which we are always falling, not backward in time, but forward toward that moment when each story, each image of God will be found, will happen again.

Marvin Hayes's art is one of imperceptible modulations among the shapes of those events we know to be visionary. These etchings are figures and places so delicately lightened, so *sewn* into being, that they seem to take place both in the human and divine worlds and in a timeless realm where only necessary things happen, and are always happening. The solid, fragile shadows, the images of God that seem always to be on the point of vanishing, are in fact—in vision—more solid than any mountain, more ever-flowing than any river. Hayes's daring hand is a steady one, and the images of God as he sees them are among the most powerful, original and compelling of our time. It is as though spiders, with their limitless and instinctive craft, had entered a human body and hand and woven out of steel these infinitely poignant images, bringing to the faces of Adam and Eve, Saul, Samson, and the glorious, sore-beset and exalted others the unforgettable qualities that they must have for us, in the lift of sunrise, the radiant stammer of noon, the grey-standing withdrawal of dusk and the deep quell of midnight. We remember.

Somerset Maugham has said in his *Summing Up*, "To my mind King James's Bible has been a very harmful influence on English prose. I am not so stupid as to deny its great beauty. It is majestical. But the Bible is an oriental book. Its alien imagery has nothing to do with us . . . those rhythms, that powerful vocabulary, that grandiloquence, became part and parcel of the national sensibility. The plain, honest English speech was overwhelmed with ornament. Blunt Englishmen twisted their tongues to speak like Hebrew Prophets."

This concept I would refute utterly. The magnificent instrument of the English language is capable of a great deal more in the way of expressiveness than the speech of "blunt Englishmen." If Dryden and Addison and Swift were our only models, English prose would tend to resemble a law brief or stockbroker's report. If it had not been for the King James Bible there would have been no Sir Thomas Browne, or, for that matter, no Thomas Wolfe, no Herman Melville, no William Faulkner, or no James Agee.

The Bible is buried and alive in us—not one of us can encounter it, and our tradition of the individual human being and the universe, who cannot but have been affected by it.

Among King James's bishops was Lancelot Andrewes, who said,

in one of his sermons, concerning the appearance of Mary Magdalene at the grave of Christ: "The Place. In the grave she saw them; and Angels in a grave, is a strange sight, a sight never seen before; not till Christ's body had been there, never till this day; this is the first news of Angels in that place. For a grave is no place for Angels, one would think; for worms rather: blessed Angels, but not in a blessed place. But since Christ lay there, that place is blessed."

One has but to glance at Hayes's etching of the Ascension to see that, through the presence of the figure of Jesus, the whole *idea* of the tomb has been, by this presence, transfigured forever in the spirit of mankind. And this is true not only for this tomb, but from that time on for all tombs everywhere. No longer are graves places to which we have been doomed, but locations from which we rise on light. The stone shall roll away, and the singing begin, and death become a story of release, reunion and fulfillment: a story of deep delight.

As for my own part, I wished to take a new approach to the events Marvin Hayes portrays and I write about. I do this in all humility, propelled by the death of my wife into a task I had long wanted to essay. She was all her life a devoted dweller in the Bible, and now, through the flowering tomb, she resides among the superhuman reality of God's images. God bless you, my good girl, bride of the first night, and now of the first light.

Old Testament

Creation

Sky. Translucent infinite acre. Anxiety of water, when the hand of God passes over it. Here in the sleep-turning void, the pain waves have not yet begun. These are the star laws, moon-turning. The infinite hands are trembling. What is coming? Sleep circles. River   eyes   dust   terror. From now will come the enormous storms over the sad volcanoes, where lava flows to no purpose. From now will come the cooling of the crust. From this the great beasts will arise; this new place will be consecrated and fertilized by gigantic blood. The ground will shake with huge lizards. In the sea, monsters slide beneath the surface, up-coming to tear other monsters apart: those swimming serenely under the hot new sun.

Why do it this way? Why the tremendous dust storms? Why the strange animals? What is to come of this? What possible end? The deep waves I have made give off nothing but meaningless, endless blood. What terror do I wish to release to the clouds I have created? I am trying something out. I don't have to do it, but the soft pain of the blue planet urges me on. This doing is precious to me. Am I ready for it? Is my only Son ready? About it and its quiet fragile air there is water, fire. There is earth. There are flowers and tenderness coming, also. It is all here, now, in my two hands. I can make the forest eagle circle over the green of leaves. I must do this thing. What I have done, I am doing. My hand passes over the deep waters, and the fish become. The forest eagle circles. Come everything. I am afraid.

Release

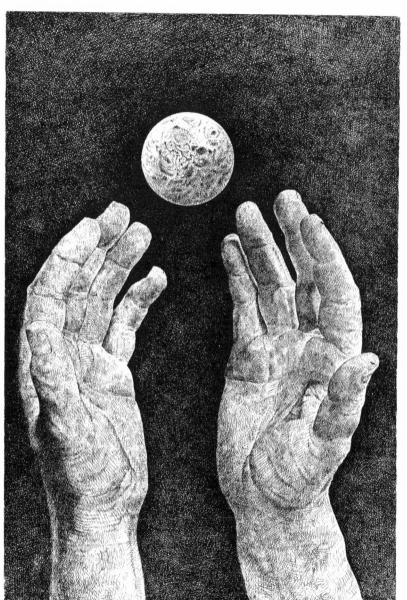

Adam

Dust fields breathe, slowly. Taking shape, the soul begins to feel its form. Around God's image tenderness begins to ache. The muscled valves of the heart begin to pulse. Adam is healed of nothingness. God murmurs over him as a mother would speak to her child, who cannot understand why he has been brought into the world, but he is there. The lids of his eyes unfold. Now there is wind upon him. The warmth of his mouth loses the last of its dust. His teeth are young. His breath is a mystical opening. His cheek and forehead find their true relationship. The great hands put him down into the world, shadows pass over him and he feels the quiet grasp of rain.

Adam hears an enormous, soft and caring voice say, "Welcome, son, creation and brother."

Brother

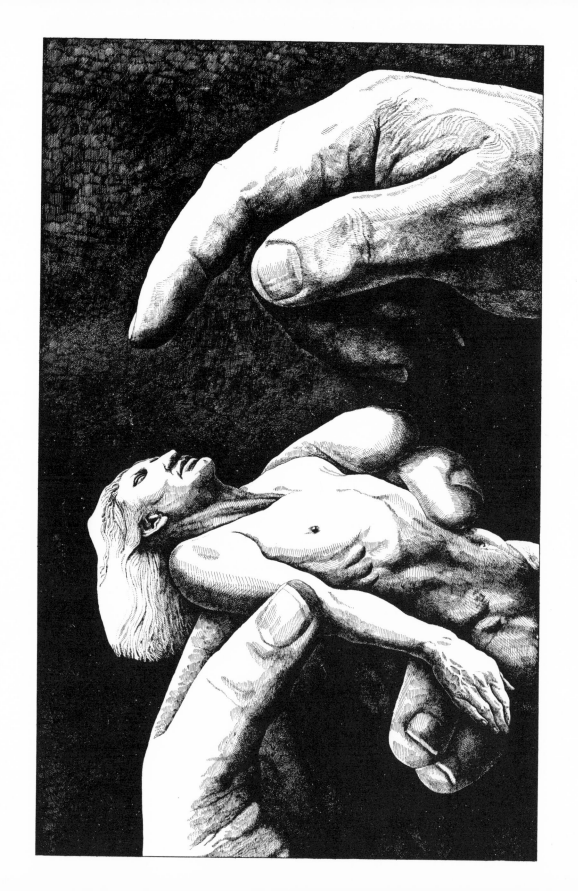

PLATE NUMBER 3 / Genesis 3 : 1
Now the serpent was more subtil than any beast of the field
which the Lord God had made. And he said unto the woman,
Yea, hath God said, Ye shall not eat of every tree of the
garden?

The Fall

My name is Eve. Around me the sunlight is rustling. There is a strange calm. My innocent eyes open on the sweet tree. There is an underground flicker, and something deadly and aggressive moves toward me. My eyes are heavy; they half open, and I am moist. There is some secret, and I know as I lie here that it will be given me. I have no need of knowledge, but I am a woman and something of deadly muscle and flickering tongue moves me as all women after me must be moved. I am unafraid. I hear without opening my eyes, and I am calm, tender and innocent. I am strange and new, but in me there is this strange voice that says eat. I will eat, and cause my husband to eat. Lightning flows through our loins.

Eat

PLATE NUMBER 4 / Genesis 4:11
And now *art* thou cursed **from the earth**, which hath opened
her mouth to receive **thy brother's blood** from thy hand.

Death of Abel

Young fear. Fear bearing deathless terror from the youth of the world. I, Cain, slew my brother Abel. Nothing is fixed; things are wandering. There is an aimless storm around me, and sheet lightning is infinite. I do not know why I did what I did, except that the force of my brother was preferred before me. Around my eternal journey among men there can be no peace; the mystery has been severed, and the curse on me has begun. Nothing like I have done has ever been done before. Abel is dead, but I must wander. I have created death and must carry it everywhere among men. My brother's death is underfoot and catches me with every footstep I take among the great cities. This all happened on a whim, and all the wars of men will come exactly thus. I bear death to men, women and children: a destruction that I do not want, for I am a gentle man.

Gentle

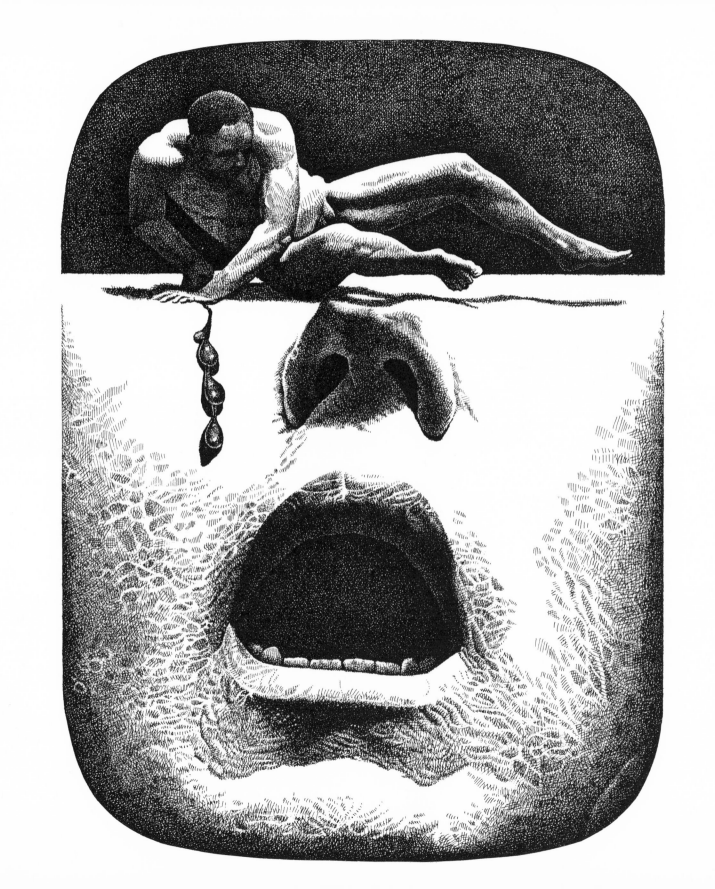

Return of the Dove

The wood sings with axes. The Lord falls when the tree falls. The Lord will lie at full length waiting to be used. He will be used as a ship. There will be the endless release of rain. The rain will strike all of the tents of men. If we do not have a sense of time, the animals and the earth will die, and fish will swim over the towers.

The vessel is precious, and the animals come to us, not out of madness, but from love. They come slowly and with a stately redemption. Around the ark the leaves steam with rain. Within the blue of the overcast, peace is pregnant with joy.

PLATE NUMBER 5 / Genesis 8:11
And the dove came in to him in the evening; and, lo, in her
mouth *was* an olive leaf pluckt off: so Noah knew that the
waters were abated from off the earth.

We set forth with the gentle warmth of animals; we know we
have recreated the earth. We must put our faith in wings, for after these
forty days and forty nights we know that God has tested us and that God
is with us. Wings are what we rely on, and they are coming. There is
land, and the terrible sustaining waters are sinking away. We have been
where no breath can be drawn, but the waters have left us and the air
is sweet. The dove lands on the horn of a deer, and softly the olive
branch is taken from its beak. We are going to live and bear our children.

Bear

PLATE NUMBER 6 / Genesis 19:26
But his wife looked back from behind him, and she became a
pillar of salt.

Lot's Wife

Beyond the brimstoning fire, the sky clears. It is still, and a woman looks back. The head turns, and in the oddly crystallizing eye the burning cities sparkle. Something is happening to her that she cannot understand. There is no escape from salt. The anonymous angels gather, and the back of her glittering hand covers her forehead. Blindness is running into her eyes. It is the blindness of salt but not of tears. She stands, waiting to crumble, with the burning cities dazzling like snow. Lost woman fixed in shimmer, departing forever into immobility and indifference. She is food for animals whose craze for salt outdoes the direct desert sun. Antelope will lick at her stillness, and the jackals will circle her and whine. The sun will leave her and come back, and the mountains will be new around her dazzling each day. Her heart is crystal noon. She stands, a virgin of salt, in her eyes the burning cities. She stands immaculate, waiting to crumble, lost in a heavenless heaven, severely, whitely

Burning

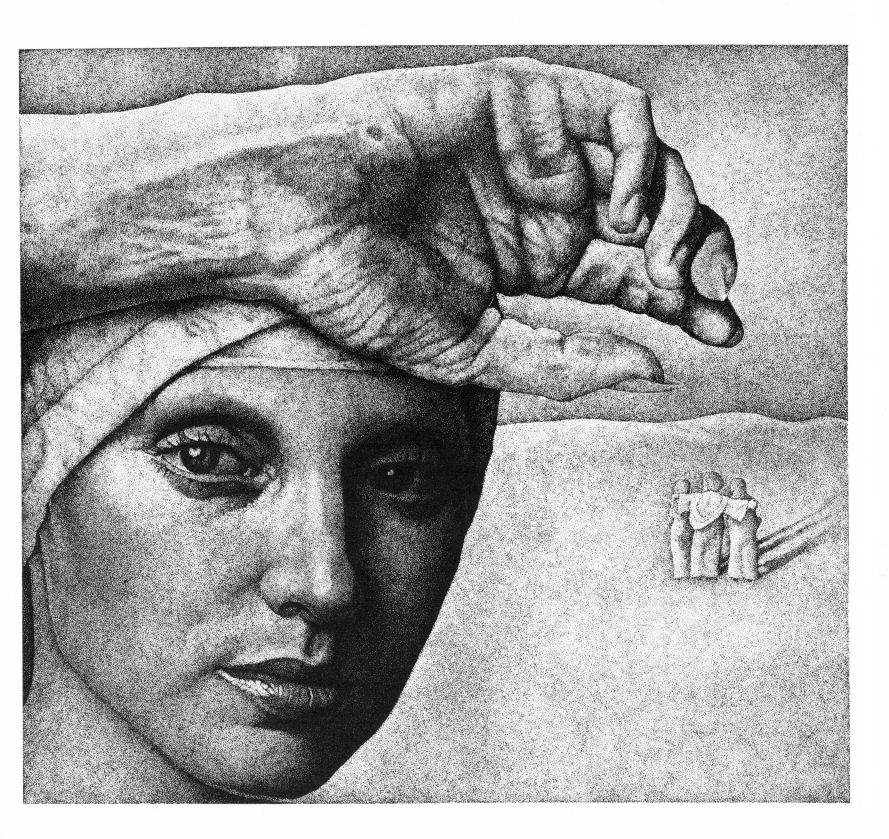

PLATE NUMBER 7 / Genesis 21:14
And Abraham rose up early in the morning, and took bread,
and a bottle of water, and gave *it* unto Hagar, putting *it* on her
shoulder, and the child, and sent her away: and she departed,
and wandered in the wilderness of Beer-sheba.

Hagar and Ishmael

The cloud of solitude stretches over the desert. Wandering of
mother and child is underneath it. Tracks of the outcasts, and also terrible
thirst. These are the slave and the prophet, and the uncertainty of
both. Can the slave rise to freedom? Can the prophet be heard? But the
great need is of water, where the sand shines like a mirror. Yet the
stones seem as though feathered with the future delight of the archer.
A disciplined kingdom is coming, if water can be found. The mother has
taken the child and cast it under a shrub. He is only a bowshot away.
And a great soft voice says, "To you and your son I will open water."
At this, at the future pointing, a bowstring vibrates like an eyelid.
There is the tension of plumed joy. An angel out of sandstone fashions a
kingdom rising. A green angel has spoken: leaves   bushes   flowers.
The kingdom of the archer is born: the dwelling in the wilderness.
The Bowman-King and the new nation

Promised

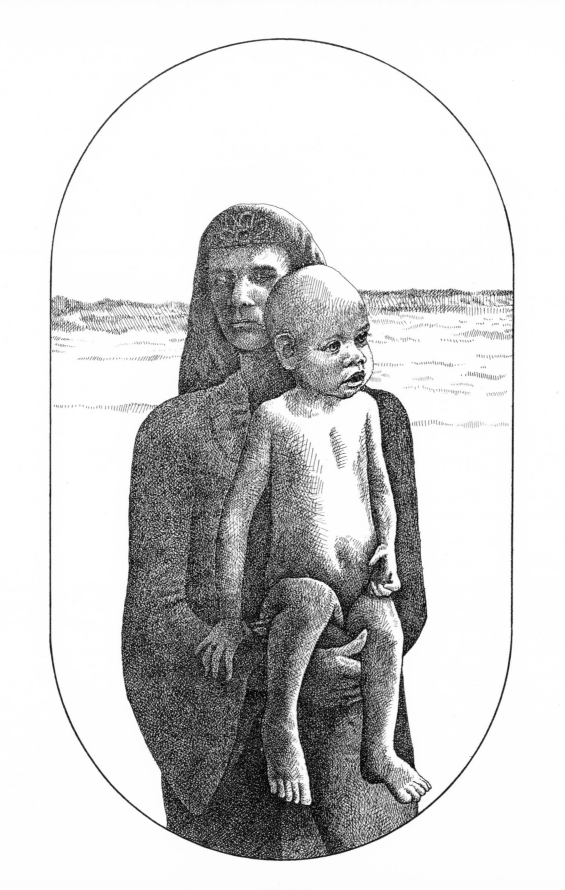

PLATE NUMBER 8 / Genesis 22:11, 12
And the angel of the LORD called unto him out of heaven, and said, Abraham, Abraham: and he said, Here *am* I.

And he said, Lay not thine hand upon the lad, neither do thou any thing unto him: for now I know that thou fearest God, seeing thou hast not withheld thy son, thine only *son* from me.

Abraham's Sacrifice

Across the throat. Son, I love you. Forgive me. Worship this cut that kills you. I am your father, Abraham; the Lord has told me to work with a glowing knife. You may cry out, but we must obey the Will. A voice has spoken across your throat, holding the knife of your father. Please forgive, my belovèd son.

   But another voice speaks. I am confused. The Word has changed, and it is now coming down through wings. It says No: this thing need not be done. The wood of the altar strains for sacrifice, but it need not be my son. The great eye of the ram is caught; there is an animal in the thicket. For my son's life, I shall burn the fleece. The rope comes off my son like the freeing of glory itself. The fleece burns, and the altar consumes itself in fire. My son is mine again. The Lord has delivered him unto his murderous father. The thicket trembles. The voice in my head is stilled by an angel. I saw him and heard him, but he has vanished into light. I know what I must do, and I know what I must not do. The burning fleece ascends. Asked for

Given

Plate Number 9 / Genesis 27:23
And he discerned him not, because his hands were hairy, as his
brother Esau's hands: so he blessed him.

Isaac's Blessing

There is a space of sand. I, Isaac, feel it with my feet. I have the
power to bless. I have one son rough with hair. Esau is far away in the
dark forest. His bowstring hums like a harp. Jacob is smooth, as a warm
stone is smooth. Someone is kneeling before me. I ask him for his
hands. They are covered with hair. Could Esau be back so soon? He is a
careful hunter. How come you are back so soon, my son? You
must have had good luck in the forest. As I hold his hand, covered with
hair like that of a goat, he is silent as he receives my blessing. I feel
the birthright pass from my blindness to my kneeling son. I hear his
knees grate in the sand and pebbles. His face is strangely smooth,
and full of soft trembling. The thing is done. Esau has my blessing. His
twin, Jacob, must perforce be the second son as he was from
his mother's womb. Nothing is false. He has good wrists, received
from God. I know him.

Son

PLATE NUMBER 10/Genesis 32:27, 28
And he said unto him, What *is* thy name? And he said, Jacob.

And he said, Thy name shall be called no more Jacob, but
Israel: for as a prince hast thou power with God and with men,
and hast prevailed.

Jacob Wrestling

I am holding a man to my breast. Brotherly, we are deep into combat.
Using all my strength, I feel through his strange body the sky descend
into the room of the night. In the blackness, I sweat like noon, and
the warm muscle against me fades in and out of my grasp. All night no
glimmer breaks, but the strength of a great antagonist flows into me.
We do not pull hair; this is no woman's work but men striving
in the dark. Whoever this is, the clutch of muscle is fine. Neither one
of us can win. Neither of us can lose. No word passes between us
until the dawn. Serene and anxious light begins to break, and I see
the long grey wings. His face is as handsome as mine, but I will not
let him go until he blesses me. "I bless thee," he says, streaming with his
athletic sweat and mine. "We have been through fighting like love."
His blessing explodes all over me. Warm combat over, he raises
his wings and smiles. I am blessed. I let him go. I kiss the palm of his
hand, and he folds his fist around it. I close my eyes and he is gone.
My name is now Israel.

Prevailed

PLATE NUMBER 12/Exodus 2:5, 6
And the daughter of Pharaoh came down to wash *herself* at the river; and her maidens walked along by the river's side; and when she saw the ark among the flags, she sent her maid to fetch it.

And when she had opened *it*, she saw the child: and, behold, the babe wept. And she had compassion on him, and said, This *is one* of the Hebrews' children.

Moses from the Nile

The flow is at the center of the world and the body of the child is moving with it. The curves of the land create the movement where the child rocks gently going toward. Fish move around the tiny boat, and the womb has not long been away. The world reveals the young sun, which is new every day as it is for all of mankind each day of its enduring life. There are girls and women among the rushes, bathing. Water streams from them and air makes the young light shine on them with innocent desire. The child, in his frail boat, is moving toward female morning. The daughter of the king is naked. Water pulses into the reeds, bearing the still child. Wet, full-bottomed and motherly, she sees the child in his frail vessel, stalled among the flag grasses, and when the child cries, she knows that the world will fulfill its promise: that she will take the river-infant in her arms and the future of men, women, families and empires will be performed. She washes the mud from her hands. Her nipples dawn. Deep in female air, she takes the child from the stream. Everything is decided. A slow breeze is found. The fresh child sleeps in her arms, and the long river takes the small boat, empty, where it must go.

River

PLATE NUMBER 11 / Genesis 37:3
Now Israel loved Joseph more than all his children, because he *was* the son of his old age: and he made him a coat of *many* colours.

Coat of Many Colors

The favorite son is in blue and yellow and red. Orange and green are on his shoulders. Lavender and gold are at his sides. Brown, aquamarine and turquoise are at his back. His father's age bursts at the same time into all colors. Flowers—tulips and jonquils, daisies, roses, and the leaves of the forest—flow, with the daffodils and orchids, into his garment from his aging father's love.

Slavery and food. He will be hated and sold by his own brothers. The coat will tatter to the winds. But he will be master of granaries and he will be the savior of an entire great people. But there will never be, for him, a still moment, an epiphany of color such as his old father has put on him in brown, violet and pink, in blood and cream and fuschia. He will die remembering how those colors fell and felt upon him.

Red

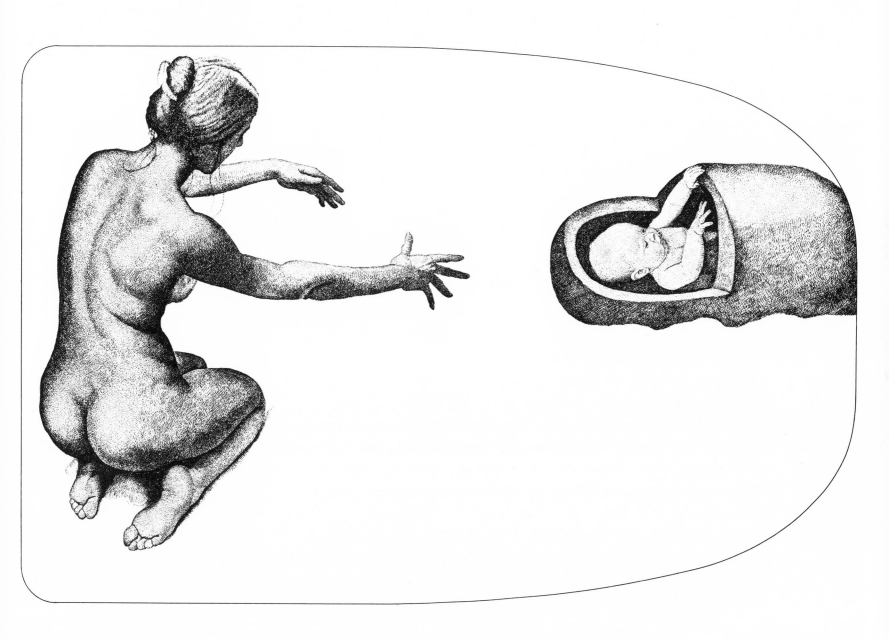

PLATE NUMBER 13 / Exodus 3:2
And the angel of the LORD appeared unto him in a flame of fire
out of the midst of a bush: and he looked, and, behold, the
bush burned with fire, and the bush *was* not consumed.

The Burning Bush

A crackling like the madness of fire-driven beasts concentrated on a single bush that burns and is not burned. God is as bright as human flame. A voice comes out of the smokeless branches. The afternoon is burning still. Egypt, the voice says. And then with a soft rustling, as of a father murmuring in his sleep, my children. Lead my children out of Egypt.

God ascends skyward, backward, back toward Himself in flame. "I am that I am," which is to say that the voice that belongs to the bush flowing upward in creative nonkilling flame is that of He that is.

Is

PLATE NUMBER 14 / Exodus 32:19
And it came to pass, as soon as he came nigh unto the camp,
that he saw the calf, and the dancing: and Moses' anger waxed
hot, and he cast the tables out of his hands, and brake them
beneath the mount.

Mount Sinai

A Hebrew cloud whirls about the mountain, hewing stone, making
tablets heavy with the laws that will tell men how to live on earth and in
heaven at the same time. The voice from the invisible contracts the
shoulder muscles of a man, and moves into his fist, holding a hammer.
The words appear unhurriedly, deeply cut around the kneeling, striking
man as sparks shower in a steady fountain of fire.

Below, as Moses descends, a calf is being formed from coins
and earrings in celebration of blasphemy. The truth of God is footing
down step by step. Incense flows over the beast of gold, and Moses
shatters the stone laws of the Lord. The words are now ten jagged slabs
of truth. The idol glitters and falls.

Truth

PLATE NUMBER 15/Deuteronomy 34:4
And the LORD said unto him, This *is* the land which I sware
unto Abraham, unto Isaac, and unto Jacob, saying, I will give
it unto thy seed: I have caused thee to see *it* with thine eyes,
but thou shalt not go over thither.

Look over Jordan

Longing for the smoke of distance. The river stands like a wall against one man who cannot cross it into his blue home, where mountains are soft with promised light, and the river that stands between a man's wild desire for his hazy, never-visited homeland is making loneliness vibrate around him like the concentric rings in water. Never has a human creature been so deeply abandoned as his people leave him and begin to cross the river into the promised land. The hushed sounds of Jericho stealthily cross the water to where the leader of his people stands waiting. Moses turns slowly away, and begins the first part of his death in the alien wilderness. Now the tribes of Israel slowly disappear into the delicate haze of the miles that lead home.

Longing

PLATE NUMBER 16/Judges 15:18
And he was sore athirst, and called on the LORD, and said,
Thou hast given this great deliverance into the hand of thy
servant: and now shall I die for thirst, and fall into the hand of
the uncircumcised?

Jawbone

The flaming foxes bolt through the rows of corn. The smoke from
their tails rises into the farm air and forms the image of a powerful man.
Forward in time from the foxes, the man slays many of his enemies.
Then his own people bind him and turn him over to those whose crops
he and the foxes have burned. There his bonds fall from him and the
Lord slays an ass and turns it to a skeleton. The jawbone is within reach
of the man favored of the Lord. He falls upon his enemies like a pillar of
fire. A thousand of them come for him and he lays about him smashing
heads, shoulders, ribs, knees. The battle surges out of the rocks and sinks
slowly to the plain where the corn had fallen to foxes. Whipsawing like a
riptide of flesh, the war of screaming men against one man with an
animal weapon spills into the burned cornfield. Samson is black with
soot, streaked with stubble smoke and blood. His enemies are sprawled
in heaps around him. Heel in eye, elbow in dead, open mouth. Men hit in
the chest have their ribs protruding like knives escaping from cages.

      All but Samson lie still. He looks at the jawbone, half-dead with
thirst, and at a word from heaven, the mouth-part that once cropped
grass fills with cool water. He drinks deep, tasting bone.

Deep

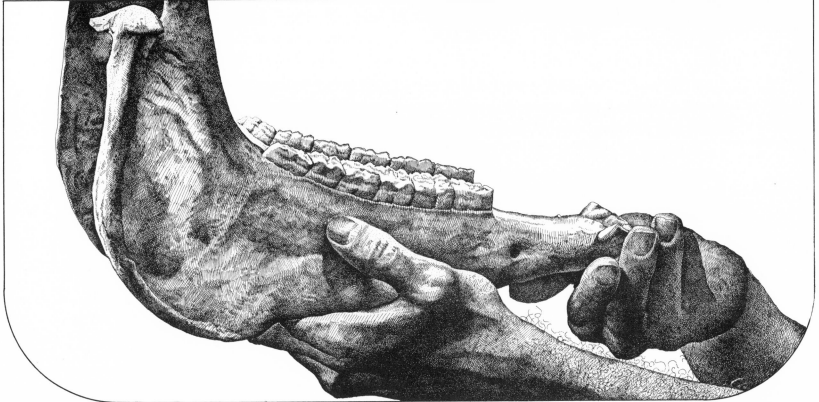

PLATE NUMBER 17/Judges 16:19
And she made him sleep upon her knees; and she called for a
man, and she caused him to shave off the seven locks of his
head; and she began to afflict him, and his strength went from
him.

Samson

A dream, not yet of loss; a dream of strength and of hunting. At the
edge of the first stream he listens and crosses into the woods. At the
second stream his head feels lighter, and dimly he can hear the clash of
sharp metal far off beyond the third stream. Wind blows and his head
feels the new cold as though ice were freezing the fourth river. There is a
feeling of ebbing in the loins. Across the sixth stream he sees a bear. He
raises the bow, pulls at the string, and it will not come back to his
cheekbone. The bushes of the forest are withered in drought; the bear he
would hunt turns away and disappears into the blasted trees as though in
contempt. He looks behind him and all seven streams are dry and wind is
cold on his head. He looks at his hands and they are trembling. Slowly he
opens his eyes where he rests on the knees of a woman. Vaguely he feels
for the seven locks of his head and tries to rise up, but he cannot move.
He looks with quivering beams into her eyes for she has said, "How
canst thou say, I love thee, when thine heart is not with me?" Dimly he
feels his heart, trying to answer. Because of you I am weak, and like any
other man.

Man

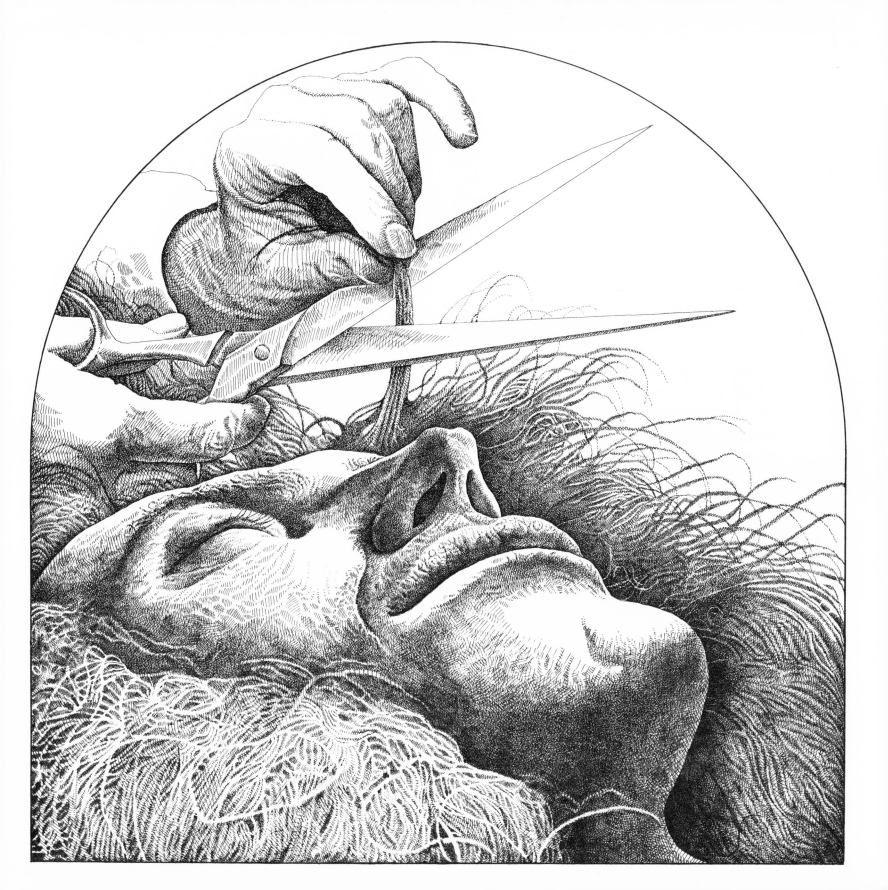

PLATE NUMBER 18 / Ruth 1:16
And Ruth said, Intreat me not to leave thee, *or* to return from
following after thee: for whither thou goest, I will go; and
where thou lodgest, I will lodge: thy people *shall be* my people,
and thy God my God.

Ruth and Naomi

Where shall loyalty end? In the desert with two women, one
moving toward an unknown destination in a strange land, but true
loyalty partakes of huge distances, of mountains and a trailless way
through rocks and sand. Each stone and each grain of sand, each desert
bush, each slope of a mountain, each head-bending ray of the sun, each
eye-lifting star of the sky pours into love and loyalty as two women toil
toward Bethlehem.

The stones and sand and sun and mountains lead into the
harvest fields of barley, where the grass is standing as it should when it is
ready for the scythe. The reaper's blade is dry and he rubs the scythe
blade with grass. The metal sings with its sharpening. At last the edge
purrs contentedly, and the reaper begins to mow, cleaving the most
secret essences of smell. The steady swings let space into the crop as Ruth
dreams of her distant place of birth. At noon she lies in the cut green, on
her gleaning arm, knowing she will marry in this place. Her loyalty will
not pass from Naomi but increase, and some of it will pass to Boaz, her
future husband, owner of fields. Naomi's gentleness will include until she
dies the mountains and the deserts of Ruth's loyalty to her, and the world
will be forever alive with the soft glow of devotion.

Forever

PLATE NUMBER 19/I Samuel 16:23
And it came to pass, when the *evil* spirit from God was upon
Saul, that David took an harp, and played with his hand: so
Saul was refreshed, and was well, and the evil spirit departed
from him.

Saul and David

Crouched inside a sore-beset and troubled king, I am eating his vitals
alive. I, too, am a spirit, dead black. My right hand is called doubt and
my left hand despair. One sickens the heart of the man wherein I dwell
and the other tears it out. Because of me, Saul will kill himself and I will
pass like night into the body of another. Soft sounds come upon me
through the body of my host. These are plucked from gut by small
fingers. They move slowly in persuasive and beautiful tones. From what
I can tell, they are the hands and the soul of a child. My dark hands are
trembling, and the heart of the man I inhabit begins to pulse with a new
strength. I must leave him in daylight, and my essence crosses the
flagstones of the balcony like a shadow. I turn to see the gentle, unhurried
boy, his fingers tangled nimbly in the strings of his harp and see the king
whom my evil would have killed, turn and behold his small savior. He
straightens and I merge my darkness with the shadows of cypress trees
and die before I can reach for another sad heart.

Heart

David

PLATE NUMBER 20/I Samuel 17:46
This day will the LORD deliver thee into mine hand; and I will
smite thee, and take thine head from thee; and I will give the
carcases of the host of the Philistines this day unto the fowls of
the air, and to the wild beasts of the earth; that all the earth
may know that there is a God in Israel.

Through sheep with a small set jaw and eyes blazing with
conviction, down a small slope, the slight boy wades into a stream and
bathes his hands in the slow movement. Without haste he picks up ten
smooth, black stones from the bed, looks at them closely and discards
five. He feels the protection of the Lord across his shoulders like the noon
sun. And the armies of the Lord upon a distant hill tremble with the
uncertainty of combat. Unhurriedly he climbs back through the sheep,
moving them gently aside with his hands to where a great cliff shaped
like a man is waiting for him. His helmet of brass towers against the
clouds and his coat of mail sparkles like the scales of a gigantic carp.
Stone is smooth in the hand and now is cradled in the sling. Slowly, as the
giant comes forward and shakes the frail boy with his footsteps, the sling
circles, moving faster, growing heavy with pull. Again, and the
thong begins a low whistling. Again, and the pitch rises until it is a
scream. At the loudest of the whistling it stops and the stone leaps from
it. Its speed is such that neither of them can see it in the air. The giant
jerks his head backwards and from it; as he falls, blood is beginning to
well. The boy walks, even strolls, to the fallen giant and draws Goliath's
anvil-heavy sword, lifts it and begins to hack as though using it to cut
through an iron-wood log. He holds up the head to both armies on their
mountains. The Lord increases David's mantle of sunlight until it burns
like the essence of courage itself. The sun that is on David's shoulders
is axe-bright.

Courage

PLATE NUMBER 21 / Psalm 23:6
Surely goodness and mercy shall follow me all the days of my
life: and I will dwell in the house of the LORD for ever.

23rd Psalm

Sheep bells keep me half-awake, but mostly I am going to sleep in
the grass with my eyes open. God holds me up in green and moves
above me in masses of slowly dissolving sky-white. It is best to see God
in the ever-changing forms of clouds, borne up at the same time by the
grass of the fields. All day I have been walking deep in nature and now I
am lying in it in the divine rest which God allows His servants. I am in
solitude, not meditating, not thinking, simply full of sunlight and my
own being. There is nothing to keep me here except a certain smile on
my face and the gentle ecstasy of doing nothing at all. This is the creative
solitude that is communion, and the good soul which is mine at
moments like this smiles with my stretched-out body, waiting for the
first sloping star, hearing water affirm the blood as it flows in my breast
as in the stream beside me. Here is the Lord's house in which I shall dwell
forever with the sheep bells wandering around me. Surely goodness and
mercy.

Surely

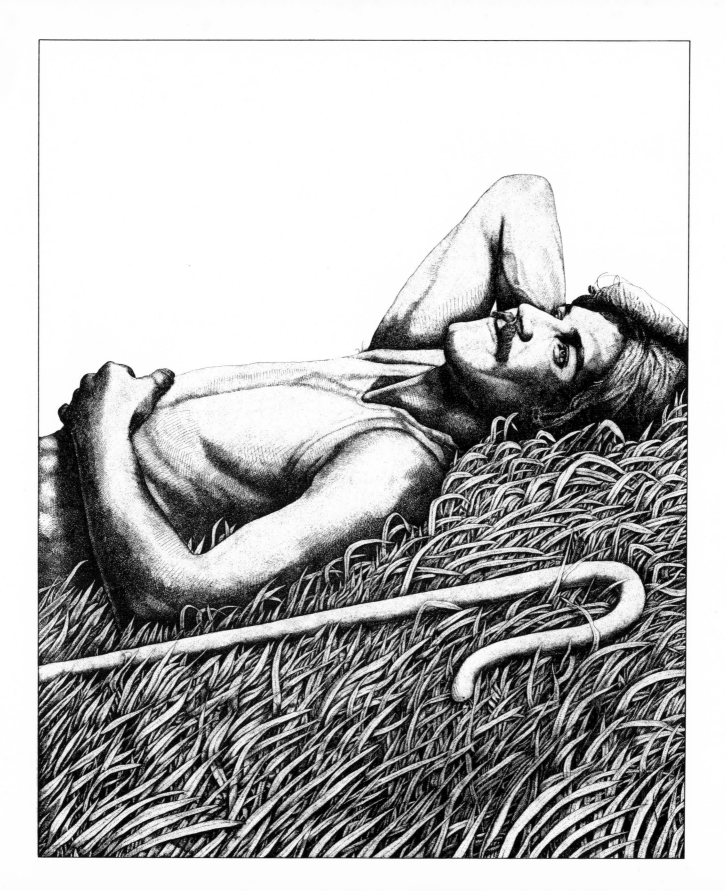

PLATE NUMBER 22 / II Samuel 18:14
Then said Joab, I may not tarry thus with thee. And he took
three darts in his hand, and thrust them through the heart of
Absalom, while he *was* yet alive in the midst of the oak.

Death of Absalom

The mule drives onward, suddenly lighter. Forked weight is gone
from him. The animal does not look back. But a man is hanging in a tree
by his hair, caught up between unattainable earth and a thick entangled
vegetated heaven, between his father and himself. The battle of Ephraim,
in which the belovèd son sided against his father, is now not even a
whisper. The only sound is the crackling of branches as a proud
rebellious boy battles against a tree, using only his hopelessly entangled
hair. Twigs have found him and lifted him from the manhood he wished
to achieve and prove against his father. The long curls are all but
grown into the branches. Blond blood pours from his scalp. His hair is so
thick that almost none of it pulls loose from his head; his forelock, still
free, now falls over his face congested with purple blood. He does not
see the approach of Joab, his father's warrior. There is a shrewd spark
through his chest, pinning him to the trunk, then another, then
the last, through his heart. His toes turn down, their arches rise in death.
His hands fall into the lower branches. The revolt of the arrogant,
honored boy is over. His father, who wanted no better son, and desired
only that Absalom be king in his stead, does not know that his greatest
hope is snarled in nature and dead by a hand the king forbade. Blood
drips from the still toes.

Later, the father—he is every father—covers his own face with his
hands, sobbing, "O my son Absalom, my son, my son Absalom! Would
God I had died for thee, O Absalom, my son, my son!"

Thee

Job

PLATE NUMBER 23 / Job 30:16, 19, 20

And now my soul is poured out upon me; the days of affliction have taken hold upon me.

He hath cast me into the mire, and I am become like dust and ashes.

I cry unto thee, and thou dost not hear me: I stand up, and thou regardest me *not*.

The dark man spoke to the Lord. "There is no man of yours I cannot turn against you." The Lord said, "I have one such. His name is Job."

        I am Job, prosperous, with good family, good crops and my health.

        I woke and looked out my window and saw that my crops were blasted as though by lightning from underneath the ground. Not a blade stood, and there was no hope for harvest. The next day I woke and my children were dead, whom I loved beyond all the telling of it. I could not say why this had befallen me. Perhaps I had offended the Lord by not enough worship and not enough prayer. So I fell to my knees and there burst blood and pus upon the floor of my home. I looked and I was covered with boils. Nothing more could afflict me. My wife cried out, "Curse God and die." But the Lord is all that I have, and all that any man asks. He is greater than the sun and the stars in heaven and if He chooses to afflict me thus, yet will I love Him. More than fields, more than sons, more than my body covered with repulsive sores, flies and insects getting at the blood. I will stand in the stillness of my affliction and live, then will walk and praise God in a shimmer of pain. The weight of sorrow is upon me. But it is nothing to the love that God bears me, and so besets and tries me. Each of my sorrows is unending praise.

Praise

Jonah

PLATE NUMBER 24 / Jonah 1:17
Now the LORD had prepared a great fish to swallow up Jonah.
And Jonah was in the belly of the fish three days and three
nights.

From the tepid having-to-make-do of the scuppers-water, from the not caring, I found myself heaved over and falling. I had no sense of the ship, but only of a deep sinking into something far vaster than I ever could have imagined. The movement was vast. I had no need of breath, but suddenly I felt a curious inward flow. I slid down a mucous tunnel and came to rest. The first thing was the smell, and the sensation that by this means I could tell the various mysteries of the depths.

I knew I was within a beast. I was sloshing in water and the water was alive: full of creatures that came from the element. I could breathe, and what I breathed was the breath of the gigantic creature that surrounded me. I was part of his food, but I was also part of the Word of God which includes all living creatures in the sea, in the air and on the land.

The greatest creation of God, the sea of the planet earth, surrounded me, and I was inside His greatest creature. The air stank with half-digestion, but I was not consumed. When the great fish rose to the surface, and left his sea breath in the air in gigantic spumes, I also exhaled: I spouted. The flesh around me was mine, stupendous as it was. It was like a cathedral of slime, arched with God's unknown, water-blowing destination. My eardrums sang far under the sea. I did not need to bless my loneliness which no man but myself has ever known. I filled the belly of the great fish, and a light shone therein. I was living in the chapel of the small and lost. And God's hand moved over the face of the day and night waters. I recovered the land and walked thereon to praise creation, and what had caused it to be, in all its forms.

Forms

PLATE NUMBER 25 / Isaiah 6:6, 7

Then flew one of the seraphim unto me, having a live coal in his hand, *which* he had taken with the tongs from off the altar:

And he laid *it* upon my mouth, and said, Lo, this hath touched thy lips; and thine iniquity is taken away, and thy sin purged.

The Calling of Isaiah

There is a six-winged rustling in the air, and Isaiah feels a strange numbness in his lips as he beholds the seraph come down with a live coal in its hand. Isaiah's lips are lifeless with lies because he, like the rest of his people, deceives. God wishes only the truth of His Word. A live coal is like the fragment of a meteor; Isaiah knows at once that his lips are to be purified by fire. His impurities of speech are to be burnt away and the seraph is with him, two wings over the eyes, two over the feet and two with which to fly. Isaiah, who would be the prophet and servant of the Most High, bends his mouth upward as though a lover awaiting a kiss and closes his eyes. His lips burn with cosmic, creative pain. The mouth burns for a long time; then the coal is taken from the charred lips. The seraph places the dying ember in Isaiah's hands and it becomes an ordinary coal. The seraph returns to the air and the six-winged rustle, like a thin breeze through an oak, disappears. But Isaiah has yet spoken no word of the Lord. Then from his black lips and tongue he begins to utter words; they are the words of a poet: holy words. Smelling the burning flesh of his own face, he goes toward his people to speak.

Speak

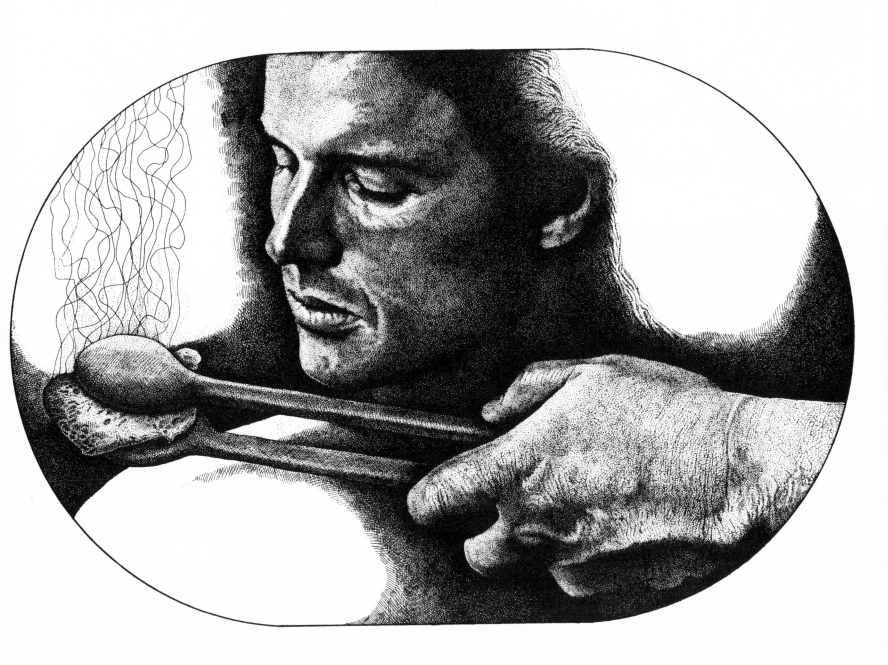

Plate Number 26/Jeremiah 19:11
And shalt say unto them, Thus saith the LORD of hosts; Even
so will I break this people and this city, as *one* breaketh a
potter's vessel, that cannot be made whole again: and they shall
bury *them* in Tophet, till *there be* no place to bury.

Jeremiah

Smooth and flawless, the pot is cradled in the arms of the prophet as
he goes toward the hardened city of Jerusalem . . . and sinful. The
people therein will suffer the siege of God through His prophet Jeremiah,
whose thunderous voice opens wide over the city, calling down the
clawed hand of God to visit its destruction on these people. The pot
is empty of everything but the city itself. It is swollen with the plagues
and diseases of sin. Jeremiah cracks the pot and the walls of the city cannot
hold. They crumble to destruction as Jeremiah's voice speaks over the
fallen gates, his ancient vision of righteousness betrayed by the wicked.
The pot is broken, the city in shambles, the people who dwelt therein all
dead. Tophet awaits them with its underground. They are buried there:
so many that there is no space in which even one more of them shall
lie. The word of the prophet and the earthen pot have combined to
punish wrongdoing. Jeremiah closes down his mighty voice and Tophet
begins to bloom in God's greenery from the bodies of sinners. Good
from evil, springing up from the renewing fields.

Fields

PLATE NUMBER 27/Daniel 5:17
Then Daniel answered and said before the king, Let thy gifts
be to thyself, and give thy rewards to another; yet I will read
the writing unto the king, and make known to him the
interpretation.

Handwriting

Let us feast, facing the wall. The chalices, the cups and the jewels change in our hands. The Temple is no longer in them, but only the use of our bodies, divorced from God. Temporarily, the wine is good. The bodies of men and women, amidst this opulence of sensuality, are good. There is the sense of glowing wealth, and the feeling that we shall pay for nothing. But slowly something is happening to us. This is no deep feast. Slowly against us is coming the judgment of the wall. We are dangling amidst the jewels, in pure terror and transgression.

Doom is tasteless. Daniel's voice speaks quietly and we stare, through the haze of our stupor, at the words telling what will happen to us. The drunken wall is blind, but words are appearing upon it. The shadow of a gigantic balance is played against the words. It tells us that we are lacking; it tells us that the Holy magic is gone from the chalices, cups and jewels we took from the Temple and used in riotous living. The writing tells us that the thought of idolatry brings nausea.

All darkness moves in on the feast. God's judgment is upon us. The balance glows with shadows, and on the blind wall of words we see ourselves descending. We had our chance. No more.

Silence

PLATE NUMBER 28 / Daniel 6:16
Then the king commanded, and they brought Daniel, and cast
him into the den of lions. *Now* the king spake and said unto
Daniel, Thy God whom thou servest continually, he will
deliver thee.

Daniel

I roam among teeth. The feline eyes are half-closed. I am not fearless
among the huge stalking shadows and the occasional white yawn.
I cannot touch these beasts, but I want to. I just stand here in a certain
brightness, among the yellow eyes. A man cannot call himself good,
under the eyes of the lions, but, praise be, I have been cast among the
animals because of good or something like it. I hear and smell the heavy
breaths around me. There is fate in my heart, but it is not obsessive.
There is no courage involved; there is only the fact of the situation
moving with the unhurried, wide pelts. Now and then, standing here,
I see the random flash of a yellow eye. The iris and pupil are astonishing,
for I stand in the dark and the eyes of huge cats behold me. I do not
remain stock-still but move a little and would like nothing more than to
place my hand deep within the mane of one of these confused creatures.
But I do not. I know that with the break of sun the angel of the Lord will
release me, and I know that what I will regret most is that I did not
touch one of these marvelous God-bewildered beasts and tell him that
I loved him, in the kingdom of all things.

Beasts

PLATE NUMBER 29 / Tobias 6:16, 17
Then the angel Raphael said to him: Hear me, and I will show
thee who they are, over whom the devil can prevail.

For they who in such manner receive matrimony, as to shut
out God from themselves, and from their mind, and to give
themselves to their lust, as the horse and mule, which have not
understanding, over them the devil hath power.

Tobias

Seven husbands sleeping. A demon melting like fog through the walls slays them one by one. The archangel Raphael takes on a disguise, slipping into the body of Azarias as though in a celestial dream of inhabiting the bodies of men. The angel, as a righteous spy in his human disguise, leads the good Tobias to do battle with the demon Asmodeus in the name of the Lord. Asmodeus flees like a burnt leaf. Raphael leaves Azarias in a flash of blinding starlight and the good man Tobias, still with the angel Raphael in his eyes and mind, marries the quiet Sara in the name of the Lord he has served.

Served

New Testament

Annunciation

Four walls, and a view of cypress trees. A girl is there with a mysterious tingling in her. She turns from the window and there is a mist in the room. This is taking shape and in it the girl senses, somewhere, wings. The figure is before her, and is slowly becoming the shape of a man. But there are wings as well. She is not equipped for such an encounter. She is gazing straight into the form of a man with wings. The wings begin to tremble without wind or any breeze. The form says to her softly, "The miracle is already forming in your womb. In you the Son of God is taking His earthly shape."

The angel Gabriel, in his nebulous form, begins to dissolve into invisibility. As he disappears, Mary, holding her hand out as though to detain the angelic spirit, feels the resolution in her loins as the angel weakens in air, leaving an empty ordinary room. But behind is a radiance of breath, an ordinary warmth become Holy.

Become

PLATE NUMBER 31 / St. Matthew 1:21
And she shall bring forth a son, and thou shalt call his name
JESUS: for he shall save his people from their sins.

Virgin and Child

He is mine, or at least half of Him is mine. Let me kiss the sweet, wet eyes that have come out of my belly. I cannot understand any of this, but I do know I hold in my lap a child who comes from me. He is the Son of God, but God needs a human mate to bring forth a human child. Gently let me rock Him and smooth down his sweaty hair. The Son of God rests easy, and the human mother rejoices deeply, as any human mother does. I love this creature come from me. I am ready for whatever may happen. The main thing is the love that I feel at this moment, and the new, dependent flesh against mine. This is the way things are and thanks be to God.

Thanks

PLATE NUMBER 32 / St. Matthew 2:21
And he arose, and took the young child and his mother, and
came into the land of Israel.

Joy

Let me embrace the utmost, the new fragility. This arm of mine is strong, from hard work, from the woodbins, from digging in the earth. Let me take this child and use my arm as a fortress against anything, any evil spirit that may come at Him. There is marvelous force in it. Lord, I am up to the protection of fragility. It is not that I have been told this is the Son of God: it could be any child and any father. This little boy has weak muscles and his eyes do not focus yet. He is subject to all diseases, and especially those of cold. I do not understand, but the flesh of the father is with this child even though You are the true Father. Humbly, I claim my human rights as the husband. Please allow the veins of my forearm to pulse with strength, daring and protectiveness.

Daring

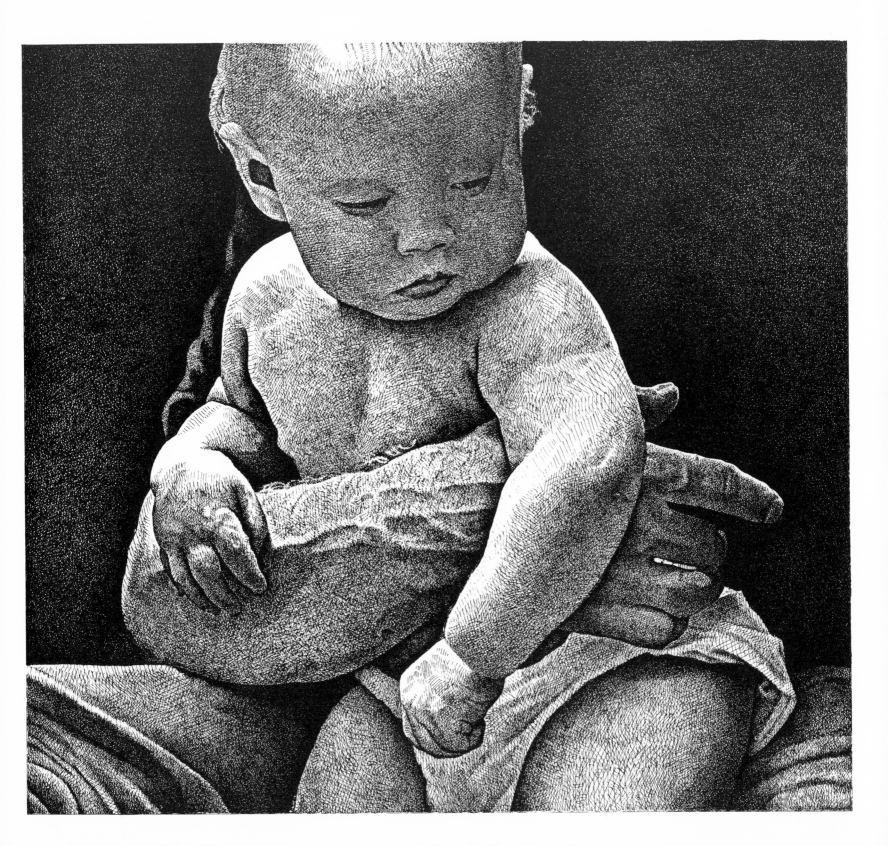

Among the Elders

The letters on the page begin to assume their true meaning; words begin to come together in the tongue of the Lord. Outside the Temple the parents are wandering, looking for their son. Old heads incline over their texts where the extraordinary boy is bringing His religion from the roots to the present moment. There is a flaw corrected; there is an image that gains strength. The knowledge of the race becomes clearer. Words are given rightly at last.

His mother and father appear in the door and speak softly. They have been worried, but the boy simply says, "I must be about my Father's business." The elders straighten, faith hovers and expands. At the center is a child.

Faith

PLATE NUMBER 34 / St. Mark 1:4
John did baptize in the wilderness, and preach the baptism of
repentance for the remission of sins.

John

Sweetness of the wilderness. I stretch my hand slowly and without
trembling among the bees. I bring forth the honeycomb and eat. There is
the play of fountains around me, and an azure nothingness which fills
with forms of men and women. They gather here to listen. A stupendous
heartbeat comes from random men as I begin to speak. I know whereof.
In the wilderness this body is alive with the sheer flame of the coming of
God. I will die for this, though I don't know where.

The shepherds come through the long leaves, and the beggars,
and I speak. I speak with the honeycomb, gentle and life-giving, in my
mouth. The brooks and rivers flow around me, and I preach the Word
which is the beginning and end of all things. Above all I preach water, for
if there is anything holy in the world, it is water flowing, standing deep
in ponds and pools, breaking on unknown beaches and rocks, as the sea
must do from the beginning of time to the end.

The Word from me breaks forth in the wilderness. Crowned
with the Coming, I see in one eye the death of Him who is greater than I,
whose advent I preach with the honeycomb. In the other, I see my own
death in which my head is severed from my body. And yet I know that
my eyes will be open, and that, mutilated, I shall still see the waters of
Jordan, still hear the sound of flowing where the sons of men will be
saved by the never-ending process of God's baptismal waters.

Saved

PLATE NUMBER 35 / St. John 9:11

He answered and said, A man that is called Jesus made clay,
and anointed mine eyes, and said unto me, Go to the pool of
Siloam, and wash: and I went and washed, and I received sight.

Healing

The delicate touch of fingertips on eyelids. I have never felt such
gentleness; creativity of the world must surely be there. There is a
pool that people will lead me to. People who care for me will know that
my eyelids are anointed. They will take me to the deep blue pool, and
divest me of my clothing. Some gentle hand, probably female, will
incline my head, so that, completely trustful, I will fall forward. After the
first shock of cold, I will arise and will see the faces of humankind.
The trees and the red flowers will be around me. I will come out of the
pool of Siloam, a man reborn among men, beholding a great world
in its magnificent colors. It is a vision every man has when he comes
from his mother's womb. I am here to affirm it. This thing has
happened. But my Master who has caused it to happen is wandering.
Where can I find Him? I cannot; but I can see.

See

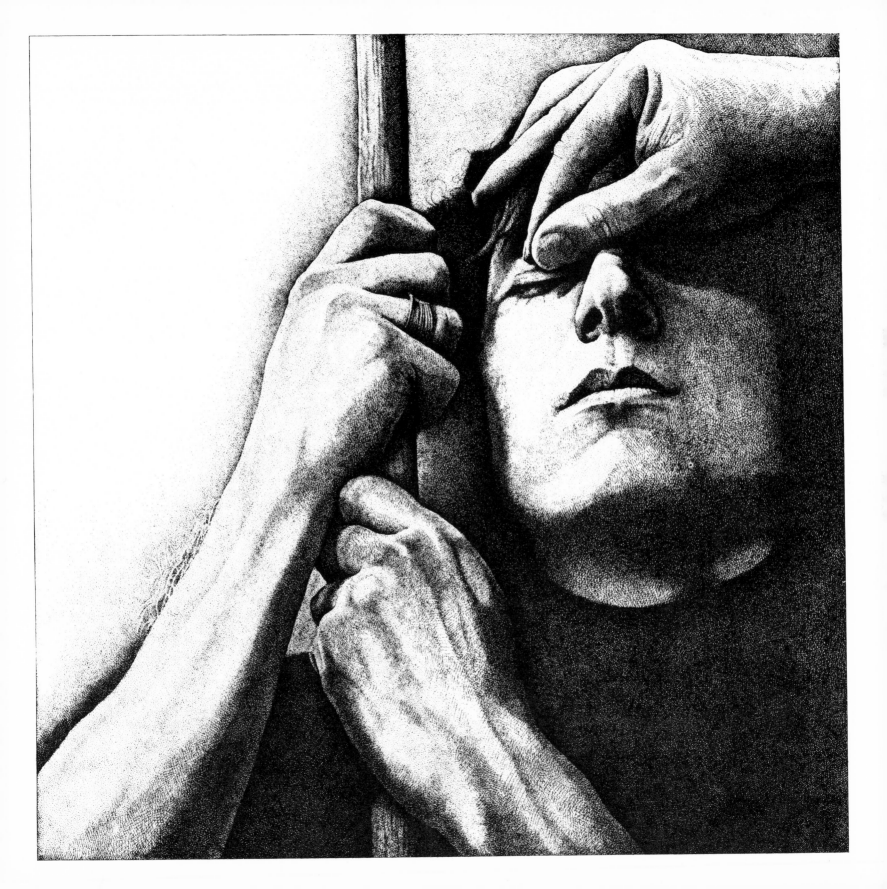

PLATE NUMBER 36/St. Matthew 13:8
But other fell into good ground, and brought forth fruit, some
an hundredfold, some sixtyfold, some thirtyfold.

The Sower

Silver day, and the epic sweep of an arm scattering the hope of life
over the earth. The sower is prodigal; any ground may have his
seeds. The prospect of bread lilts downward through the air, and blows
upon the wind. Some seeds fall upon stone and lie sterile, some are
enmazed among thorns and never reach the earth, some are devoured by
animals, some caught in the hornbills of birds, and are lifted to death
in the air. Yet there is good ground, and when the sower's seeds fall
upon it, the rain, the sun, and the earth will give the best of themselves.
This ground has been prepared deep in the curve of the cycle,
and will make life.

Prepared

PLATE NUMBER 37/St. Matthew 17:2
And was transfigured before them: and his face did shine as the
.sun, and his raiment was white as the light.

Transfiguration

For no reason our Brother bids us go with Him to the high, the solitary mountain. We follow wordlessly. We know that He would not ask us to go with Him if it were not important. It is not a difficult journey, though each leg grows tired at the continual ascent. Then the trees break, and He beckons us to be separate from Him. We wait in bushes, and He waits alone. His face is as of the ground where there are shadows. Then, slowly, His countenance rises through the shadow, through the shade cast by leaves into the utter blackness of midnight.

We, His brothers, can see enough to know that there is a cloud passing over the central darkness of the moon. We see Him with His hands in a gesture of utter acceptance. He is our Brother. We do not know Him, but we will follow Him to the death. We will follow Him to the moonlight on the mountain.

A great light, as that of noon, breaks slowly upon His form. We feel on our faces a radiance that is not ours. From somewhere deep within the sky, from somewhere above, from the heart of a small cloud, a voice is over us, saying, "This is my beloved Son, in whom I am well pleased."

Voice

PLATE NUMBER 38 / St. Luke 13:6, 7, 8, 9

He spake also this parable; A certain *man* had a fig tree planted in his vineyard; and he came and sought fruit thereon, and found none.

Then said he unto the dresser of his vineyard, Behold, these three years I come seeking fruit on this fig tree, and find none: cut it down; why cumbereth it the ground?

And he answering said unto him, Lord, let it alone this year also, till I shall dig about it, and dung *it*:

And if it bear fruit, *well*: and if not, *then* after that thou shalt cut it down.

Christ and the Fig Tree

There must be *prepared* soil.

All growth and life and vitality come from it. As it is with the soil, so it is with the soul.

All things must die properly.

The fruit of the fig tree rises freely. The growth is just. But, the Son of Man said that the sinner must repent and bear fruit, or die. And die merely, and feed the soil. Or the man must die, flower, and live again, as the tree blooms.

Grow

PLATE NUMBER 39/St. Luke 15:20
And he arose, and came to his father. But when he was yet a
great way off, his father saw him, and had compassion, and
ran, and fell on his neck and kissed him.

Prodigal Son

Home. I do not know where my son has wandered, but he is home.
His return makes me feel like a god, so that I would do anything—
anything in the world for him. My son is *Home*! I do not yet know
where his feet have trod, over what seas he has sailed. The main thing is
that he is once again in my arms. That he has returned. "Son, hold
my hand, and feel my years of pity for your wandering." As father, let
me do what I can. Let me make the festivities for the wanderer. Surely
his brother will understand. He has come back to God as though to his
own earthly father. But no heavenly father could feel the marvelous sense
of recovery that I feel as I hold his battered head in my arms. My son
has come home. Let us throw wide the windows of the house. Let us
feast, and let me not be far from holding his hand or his head.

Feast

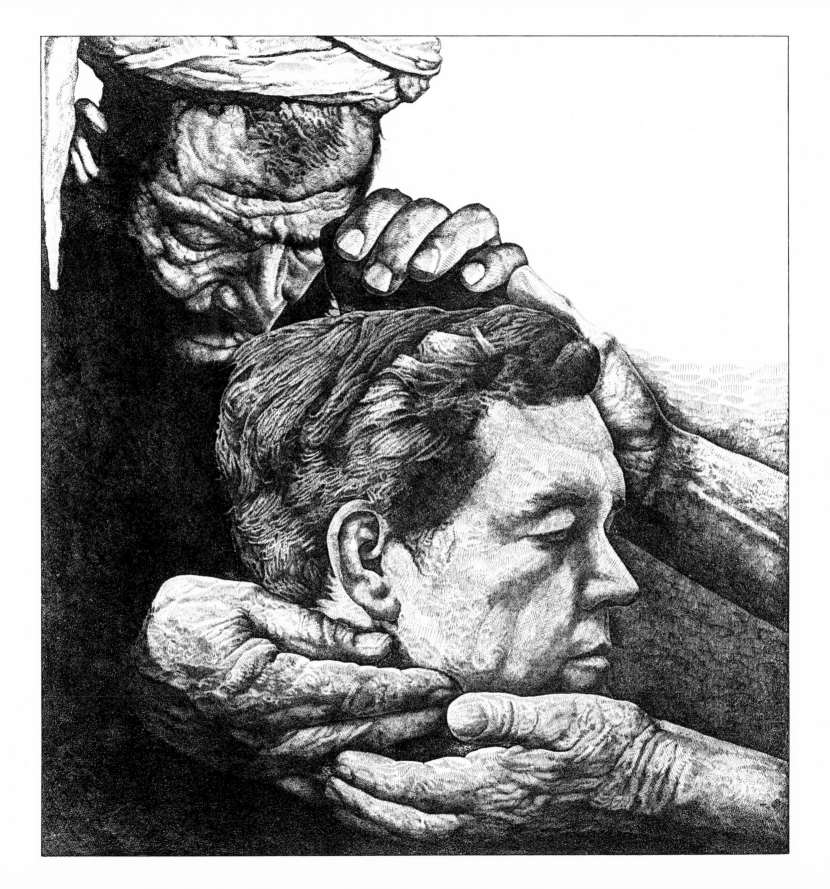

Plate Number 40/St. John 11:43
And when he thus had spoken, he cried with a loud voice,
Lazarus, come forth.

Lazarus

All silence. Memory tries. More silence, and this will go on.
Memory is struggling. I am very cold. I am wrapped in something.
I might be able to move. I am not able to try yet. I will not try. Maybe
later. My mouth is full of dryness. It might be dust, it might be sand,
or simply the taste of nothingness itself. I have been dead. But something
is happening to me that all the dead long for.

      I smell the decay that is my own. My nose is underground.
I can inhale, and what enters my lungs is the sweat of interior stones. But
somehow the air is becoming sweet. Someone is tapping on thick
stone. I hear a voice saying, "Come forth." Light strikes me full in the
forehead and I open my eyes. Through the cloth over my head, I see
a man of infinite gentleness come toward me crowned with new leaves.
I cannot tell which is He, or which is the sun itself. A voice bids me
to rise and come forth. I do, and I am alive.

Alive

PLATE NUMBER 41 / St. Luke 22:14
And when the hour was come, he sat down, and the twelve
apostles with him.

The Last Supper

Darkness, with spread-upward light. Men are embarked on something mysterious. Jesus is like them, and they can understand Him deeply on the basis of His manhood. But He is also profoundly different, giving them an inkling of what men through God may *become*. Something terrible is working in a simple meal: something terrible and wonderful.

Bread and wine. Eating and drinking are simple things. Immortality is simple. Under these strange circumstances the eating of the common bread and the drinking of the common wine will stand for immortality through a great terrifying and liberating pain.

The key is humbleness. The Son of God does not abase Himself, but He *ministers*. That is the true meaning of all of His teachings. You *minister* to the *other*. Any wellspring of human kindness—always available—can flow over into another human being. You are humble before all humanity, and will wash feet.

Humble

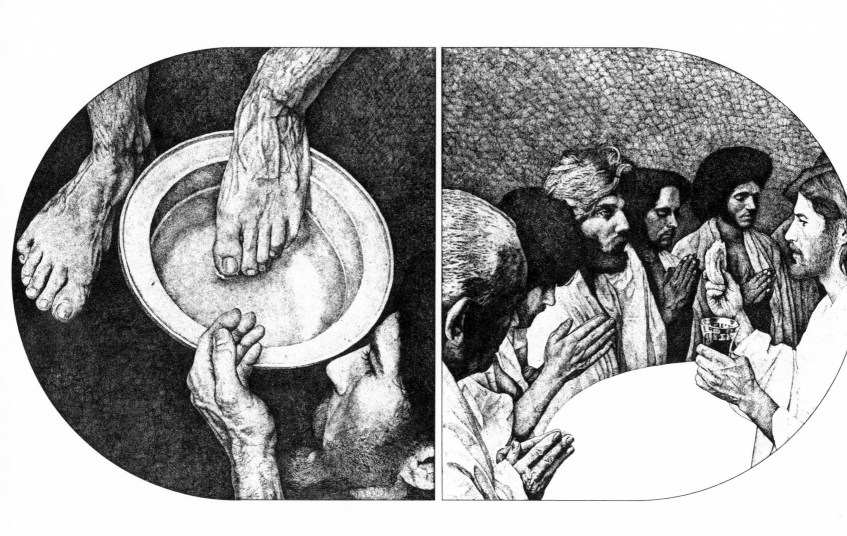

PLATE NUMBER 42 / St. Mark 14:21
The Son of man indeed goeth, as it is written of him: but woe
to that man by whom the Son of man is betrayed! good were
it for that man if he had never been born.

Judas

C oins.

These are heavy in my hands.

Silver is heavy, and the profile on them is part of the weight. These are
Caesar's heads, and they come through an occupied people. These people
are my people.

I have betrayed my Lord for these.

Why?

I had no choice, and know I have no way but death to prove
my inexplicable love; no way but a rope and a leaning tree.

I stand condemned in all histories.

But what I want to do is one kind act. Please, God, if You love
me for doing Your strange will, show me one beggar, one incurably
old woman or man to whom I can make a difference, and then let me
hang myself as I must do. Know, Father, as I place the hemp around my
neck, and scatter the Caesar-headed coins, that I am Thy servant.
My name is Judas, and I am dying for You.

Servant

PLATE NUMBER 43 / St. Matthew 27:29
And when they had platted a crown of thorns, they put *it* upon
his head, and a reed in his right hand: and they bowed the knee
before him, and mocked him, saying, Hail, King of the Jews!

Flagellation

My head is encircled by a forest. The forest is pointed and comes
from the lowest of bushes. There are heavy straps across my back. My
Father in heaven, how could You let this be done to me? My brain
is alive with the sharpest things that have sprung out of the ground.
My back is suffering terribly from the hide of the ox.

> *Why*, Father?
> I have come to the earth as Your son, as the only Son of God.
> But I am suffering pain as a man.
> Pain.
> This must be what was intended, but *why*?

> Why?

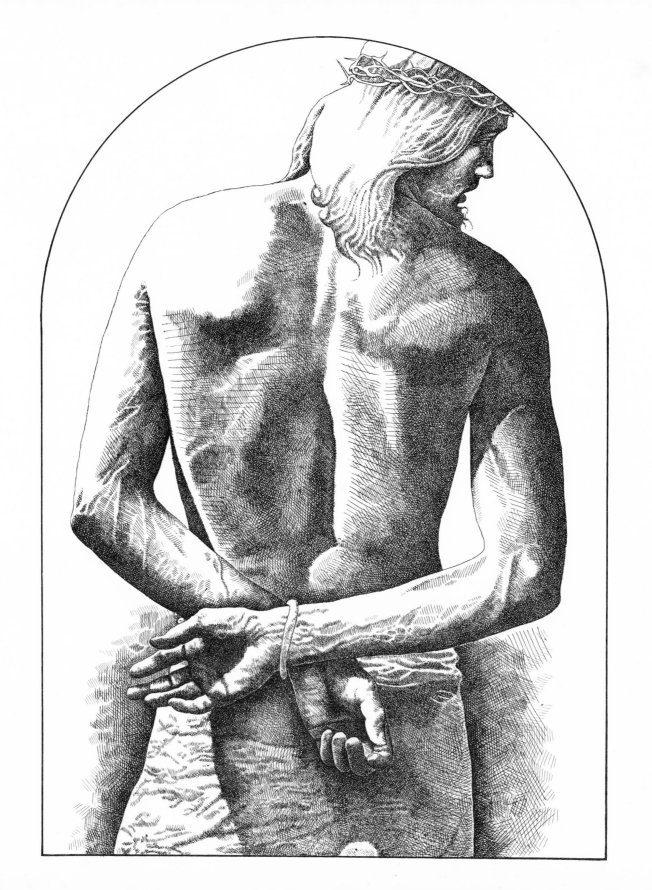

PLATE NUMBER 44 / St. Matthew 27:32
And as they came out, they found a man of Cyrene, Simon by
name: him they compelled to bear his cross.

Simon

Fear like a dancing of peoples. Slavery. Wood is put upon my back which suddenly seems to be made for it. Labor, pantingly, understood. I, a black man, am pressed into the rough shape of a cross. Sweat is very heavy. Weight, hard. Let us do our best, black skin or white, to get up a hill with our load. Something not mine, but hot and dusty, is going to happen. I am black. But if I can know the shape of this hill, it will be mine, too. I have the experience in my back of splinters, and the shape and weight of something important. I may stagger, but I will not fall. I understand, no matter what.

Splinters

No Greater Love

What is this?

My own terrible death. And it *will* be terrible; I know it already. It is very heavy.

Rough wood, confusion and pain.

I cannot understand why all these people are around. What have I ever done that there should be such crowds to see me die?

Something kicks me. It may be a man or an animal.

Everything is against me. I cannot carry this thing much farther. They will have to carry me. There is this awkward torture, dragging. There are my own horrible hands, which are not hands anymore. Blistered confusion of back and feet. Where they tell me to go, I shall go. There is no other way to my Father.

Carry

PLATE NUMBER 46/St. John 19:25, 26

Now there stood by the cross of Jesus his mother, and his mother's sister, Mary the *wife* of Cleophas, and Mary Magdalene.

When Jesus therefore saw his mother, and the disciple standing by, whom he loved, he saith unto his mother, Woman, behold thy son!

Pietà

In the deep fluids of sight a man is hanging. He is my Savior.

I am His mother.

Can such things be?   Yes.   The lashed round of the eye sees Him hanging. He is there and nowhere else. I think I must help to take Him down. There is a sense of darkness, and time. After that I have no idea. It may be that nothing will change. But it might also be that strange, almost miraculous things will happen.

A man is hanging on a cross, blood pouring down Him, but I stand here as a woman, and I do not believe that this is the end for Him or for any of us.

End

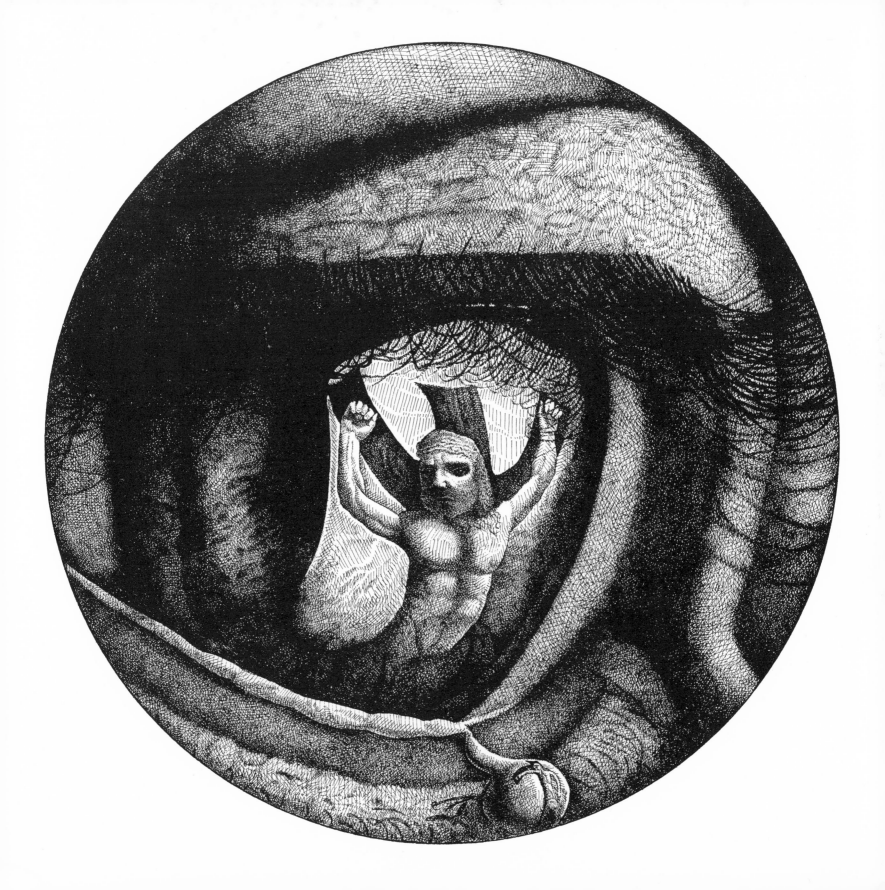

PLATE NUMBER 47/St. John 3:16
For God so loved the world, that he gave his only begotten
Son, that whosoever believeth in him should not perish, but
have everlasting life.

For God So Loved the World

My Lord and Father, let me be total. I am a human being and I have gone through pain, and exaltation. I have known poverty, suffering and the great strength of the human word called poetry. Through all of these things runs the knowledge of my Father, though what His true Will, none can say. I stand in the proud light and the muscles of a man stand up within my body and rise toward brilliance. In one moment I can say anything.

Light

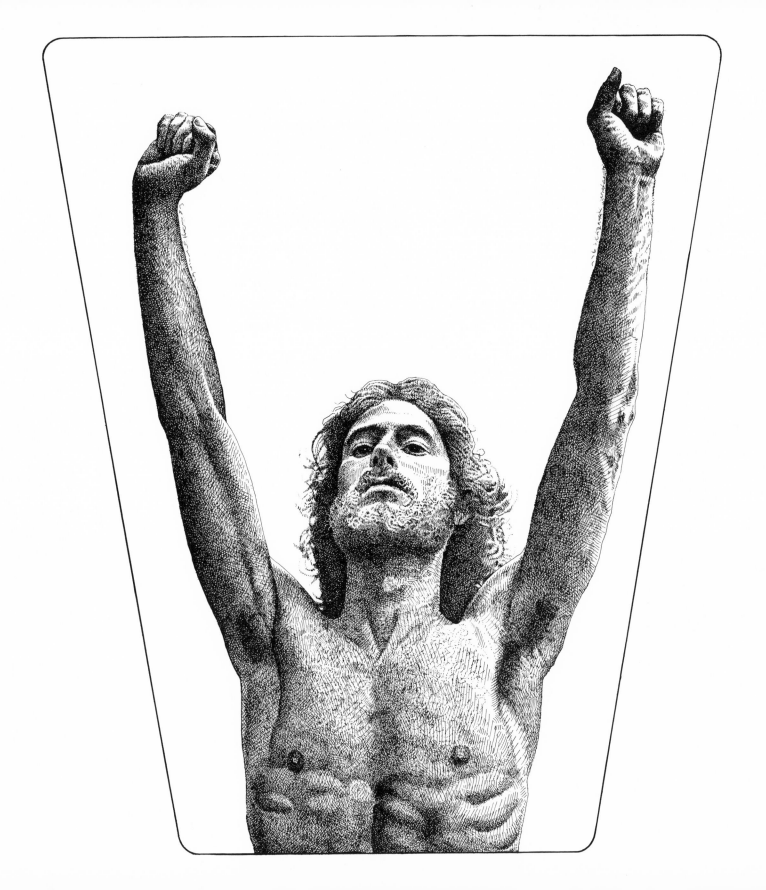

PLATE NUMBER 48 / ACTS 1:9
And when he had spoken these things, while they beheld, he
was taken up; and a cloud received him out of their sight.

The Ascension

Very gently He touched my neck, and felt the blood throb there.
In that touch there was infinite love, and no question. He looked upward
toward blueness, across which a cloud was beginning. I tried to hold
Him in my arms, but somehow knew this was not the time to
restrain Him.

He lifted away from me easily.

I held His warm, humanly-pulsing ankle in my hand as He
went slowly upward. He entered the cloud.

He was gone from us, and never gone.

Never

PLATE NUMBER 49 / St. Mark 16:19
So then after the Lord had spoken unto them, he was received
up into heaven, and sat on the right hand of God.

Jesus Laughing

To any laugh, the stones of anywhere respond. Is this a trick?
Are time and pain in it? Is ease in it?

Now where I am laughing, what keeps the balance? Sunset,
probably. Also the leaves and animals and the sound of birds in the air
that would all be disappointing if it were not all so glorious at this
time of day. There should have been a disappearing act; there should have
been teasing and the fun of "let me show you something new." My
Father granted me laughter, in the insects and the flowers. Men speak
of me as a man of pain and sorrow, but they have not reached the other
side of God, and while I was here among you, the pain and terror
were balanced by a good deal of teasing that nobody believed but God;
by a great grin into nothingness, which justified everything; by a strong
measure of sly Holy fun.

Laughter

PLATE NUMBER 50/ ACTS 9:3, 4
And as he journeyed, he came near Damascus: and suddenly
there shined round about him a light from heaven:

And he fell to the earth, and heard a voice saying unto him,
Saul, Saul, why persecutest thou me?

Paul

I hated all of them. I hated this secret knowledge that they might
possess. These Christians seemed to me dangerous, and so I attempted to
diminish their numbers as best I could.

I did not understand; I understood nothing of love.

But I was walking on a road. I had no business going to
Damascus. But suddenly I fell to my knees for some reason I cannot
even yet understand. A huge light filled my brain. I would die in Rome,
a martyr. God had found me walking the road to Damascus, and I would
be in the ever-living light of heaven forever, no matter what happened
to me on earth.

Forever

PLATE NUMBER 51 / Revelation 8:10, 11

And the third angel sounded, and there fell a great star from heaven, burning as it were a lamp, and it fell upon the third part of the rivers, and upon the fountains of waters;

And the name of the star is called Wormwood: and the third part of the waters became wormwood; and many men died of the waters, because they were made bitter.

The Third Trumpet

Seven winged trumpeters take their places in the void, and now the third of these presses the dark instrument to his lips. In the sound are the bellowing of bulls through their horns, the sliding of huge masses of ice into frozen seas, the screams of impaled lions, the terror of small children at midnight, the convulsive groaning of earthquakes and the storm-sounds of herds fleeing forest fires. In answer, a great star slowly shines itself into being, brighter and brighter until all sight draws backward into the head. Slowly the star begins to fall, and then soundlessly explodes. Its blue-white fragments splinter downward, heading for rivers. Men open their eyes, blind now not with light but with thirst. Rivers flow in the calm moonlight. They move in this celestial light as they have always done, but they have been changed from within. A man lifts from an ancient riverbed a double handful of water, and drinks because he must. Now he lies in a strange, unforgiven position. He is dead. Above him the third trumpet still sounds, curving back over the head of the angel.

Curving

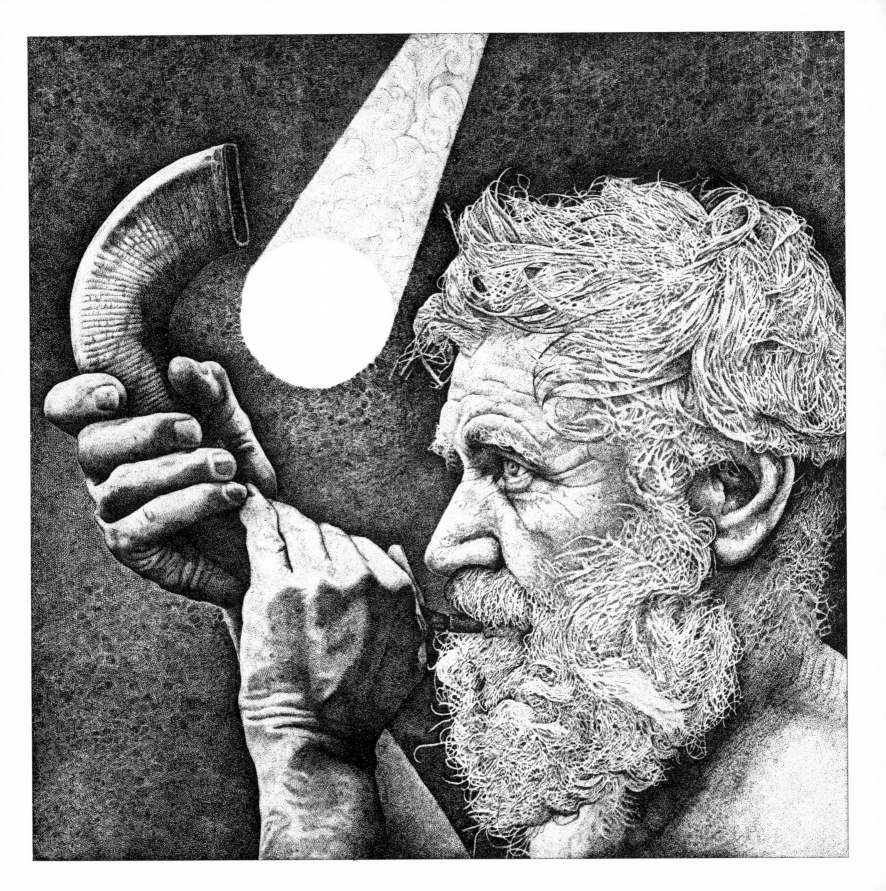

PLATE NUMBER 52 / Revelation 1:7
Behold, he cometh with clouds; and every eye shall see him,
and they *also* which pierced him: and all kindreds of the earth
shall wail because of him. Even so, Amen.

The Second Coming

Returned. Return. Oh my God, Father!

All praise.

I know this place, and the fields open deeply before me in flowers, the sun is bursting with life on my shoulders and I have come back to the place You sent me. There is no blade of grass before me that I cannot bless or that You have not given to the grace of living things. I walk among them, knowing that men will understand me now. I am total, as I return. Bless You, Father, for making this world.

I was created to be here. Let the sun flow upon me and the flowers start up in great bunches at my feet in the wide field. No matter what happens to me now, I have returned, praise God. This is my earth. I have returned.

Returned

Return

Afterword

Release me to thee, my brother; your gentle burning was promised and now is given to a son who has prevailed by the red river in deep longing, and the heart which has served thee with courage will speak to wrongdoers; all those who condemn silence to death and bear witness to the beast-forms of the saved will be wandering with thanks grown endless: we are all daring with faith and laughter, and seed feasts in splinters under everyman's feet now; see the voice that saves and eats and is given to the burning servant—carry light, become the end, return forever with borne glory, give thanks and ask

why?

Catalogue of Etchings

Etchings are listed consecutively as they appear in the book.
Sizes shown are in inches, with vertical measurement first.